WITHDRAWN

The Biography of Rubber

Carrie Gleason

Crabtree Publishing Company

www.crabtreebooks.com

Crabtree Publishing Company
www.crabtreebooks.com

For my dad, Ross

Coordinating editor: Ellen Rodger
Series editor: Carrie Gleason
Editor: Adrianna Morganelli
Design and production coordinator: Rosie Gowsell
Cover design and production assistance: Samara Parent
Art direction: Rob MacGregor
Scanning technician: Arlene Arch-Wilson
Photo research: Allison Napier

Photo Credits: AP/ Wide World Photos: p. 25 (bottom), p. 30 (bottom); Private Collection, Archives Charmet/ Bridgeman Art Library: p. 4; Private Collection/Bridgeman Art Library: p. 20 (bottom), p. 26; Private Collection, The Stapleton Collection/ Bridgeman Art Library: p. 17 (top); Paul Almasy/ Corbis: p. 6; Bettmann/ Corbis: p. 21 (bottom), p. 24; Corbis: p. 16; DK Limited/ Corbis: p. 23 (bottom); Gustavo Gilabert/ Corbis Saba: p. 1, p. 9 (top right); Wolfgang Kaehler/ Corbis: p. 17 (bottom); Earl and Nazima Kowall/ Corbis: p. 27 (top right); Lake County Museum/ Corbis: p. 31 (bottom); Jacques Langevin/ Corbis Sygma: p. 27 (bottom); Modesto Bee/ Corbis Sygma: p. 29 (bottom); Stephanie Maze/ Corbis: p. 25 (middle right); Steve Raymer/ Corbis: p. 8; Jeffrey L. Rotman/ Corbis: p. 28; Rykoff Collection/ Corbis: p. 14 (top); G.E. Kidder Smith/Corbis: p. 5 (bottom); David Woods/ Corbis: p. 3; Michael S. Yamashita/ Corbis: p. 7; Getty Images: cover; Bert Hardy/ Picture Post/ Getty Images: p. 10 (bottom); Hulton Archive/ Getty Images: p. 19 (top center); Robert Yarnall Richie/ Time Life Pictures/ Getty Images: p. 11 (bottom); Sasha/ Getty Images: p. 13 (bottom); Sandro Tucci/ Time Life Pictures/ Getty Images: p. 10 (top); The Granger Collection: p. 14 (bottom), p. 15, p. 23 (top); SSPL/ The Image Works: p. 5 (top), p. 9 (top left), p. 18, p. 19 (middle right), p. 29 (top), p. 30 (top right), p. 31 (top); NRM/ SSPL/ The Image Works: p. 22; North Wind Picture Archives: p. 12; Anti Slavery International/ Panos Pictures: p. 20 (top); Other images from stock photo cd.

Cartography: Jim Chernishenko: p. 7

Cover: New tires move along a conveyor belt at a factory in Napanee, Ontario, Canada.

Title page: A rubber worker rolls a ball of natural latex on the end of a long poll. The latex will later be further processed to make rubber goods.

Contents: Most bathtub rubber ducks are made from plastic today, but still retain the name of the commodity they were made from originally.

Crabtree Publishing Company

www.crabtreebooks.com   1-800-387-7650

Cataloging-in-Publication Data
Gleason, Carrie, 1973-
    The biography of rubber / written by Carrie Gleason.
        p. cm. -- (How did that get here?)
Includes index.
ISBN-13: 978-0-7787-2486-5 (rlb)
ISBN-10: 0-7787-2486-7 (rlb)
ISBN-13: 978-0-7787-2522-0 (pbk)
ISBN-10: 0-7787-2522-7 (pbk)
    1. Rubber--Juvenile literature. I. Title. II. Series.
TS1890.G53 2005
678'.2--dc22   2005019025
                                                              LC

**Published in
the United States**
PMB 16A
350 Fifth Ave.
Suite 3308
New York, NY
10118

**Published
in Canada**
616 Welland Ave.
St. Catharines
Ontario, Canada
L2M 5V6

**Published in the
United Kingdom**
73 Lime Walk
Headington
Oxford
OX3 7AD
United Kingdom

**Published
in Australia**
386 Mt. Alexander Rd.
Ascot Vale (Melbourne)
VIC 3032

Contents

The Sap of a Tree

Countless everyday objects are made from rubber. Rubber is used in the transportation and manufacturing industries in tires, belts, hoses, and many other machine parts. We even wear rubber in our clothing. In the garment industry, rubber is used to make stretchy fabrics and elastic. The world's desire for rubber is so great that fortunes have been made, cities founded, and lives have been lost, on the production and trading of this important commodity.

Rubber Supply

Rubber is a valuable commodity, or trade product, that is bought and sold around the world. In its raw form, natural rubber is called latex. Latex is a sap produced by certain plants and trees, including the rubber tree. People gather and process latex, and make it into rubber.

▶ *The workers in this old postcard image are tapping rubber trees for latex sap. Latex sap is produced by many plants but the rubber tree, native to the Amazon rainforest of South America, is the source of the best latex for making rubber.*

Rubber Demand

Rubber is used to make goods because of its special characteristics, such as **durability**. Rubber is stretchy and waterproof. It relaxes back to its original shape after being stretched out, while remaining strong. At one time, the demand for rubber was so high, and the supply so low, that scientists came up with an artificial type of rubber, called synthetic rubber, to replace natural rubber. There are now many kinds of synthetic rubber that suit different uses.

▸ *This rubbber test dummy has been filled with water to make it as heavy as a human. Rubber dummies are used to test car safety and airplane ejection seats.*

(above) The demand for rubber tires for vehicles expanded the rubber market in the early 1900s, and made some tire manufacturing centers famous throughout the world.

What Is Rubber?

Most of the world's natural rubber comes from the *Hevea brasiliensis,* or rubber tree. The tree is native to Amazonia, an area of land in South America surrounding the Amazon River and the rivers that drain into it. The rubber tree is one of thousands of species of trees and plants native to the rainforest. Eight countries in South America, including Colombia, Ecuador, Peru, and Brazil, claim parts of Amazonia. At one time, almost all natural rubber came from Amazonia, especially from Brazil. Today, most of the rubber from Amazonia is used only in South America.

The Rubber Belt

The rubber tree is a **tropical** tree. Most rubber trees are grown in a "belt" around the earth that is within 700 miles (1100 km) north and south of the equator. Today, rubber trees are grown in the tropics of Africa, Central and South America, and Southeast Asia. The countries that produce most of the world's rubber are Thailand, India, Indonesia, and China. Other big producers are Vietnam, Liberia, Brazil, Malaysia, Cambodia, and the Philippines. Most natural rubber used today is mixed with synthetic rubber. The countries that use the most rubber are China, the United States, and Japan. About 65 percent of all rubber used today is synthetic rubber.

(right) Rubber trees, planted in uniform rows, are tended by tappers on a Malaysian plantation. Malaysia is one of the world's largest rubber producers.

Disease in Rubber Plantations

The biggest threat to natural rubber production today is the South American leaf blight. This is a fungus, or disease, that spreads quickly between rubber trees that are planted too close together. Rubber trees in South America cannot be grown on plantations because of this leaf blight. Instead, rubber is harvested from trees that grow wild throughout the rainforest. The leaf blight fungus spreads by releasing **spores**, which are carried from tree to tree by the wind. Infected trees first show signs of the disease on their leaves, which turn gray and die. Eventually, the whole tree dies. The disease has not yet spread to Southeast Asia. If the disease did spread to plantations in Southeast Asia, scientists estimate that all the rubber trees would die within five years, ruining the natural rubber producing economy of those areas.

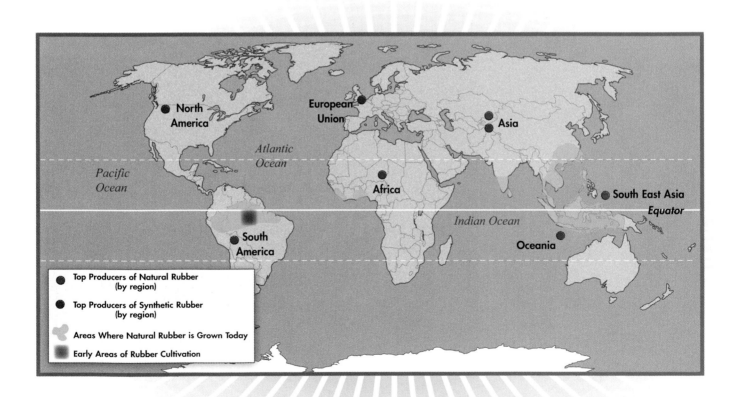

The top producers of natural rubber are located in tropical areas of the world. Synthetic rubber is produced in factories.

The Science of Rubber

There are ten species of *Hevea* plants, all of which belong to a family, or larger group, called the *Euphorbiaceae*, or spurge family. Another common plant in this family is the Manihot plant, which is the source of a pudding called tapioca. Poinsettias, plants usually associated with the **Christian** holiday of Christmas, are also members of this family. Most members of this plant family produce a milky sap.

Latex Sap

The milky sap that oozes from *Hevea* plants when they are cut is called latex. *Hevea* plants form latex in a process called biosynthesis. The plants take in non-living **nutrients** from the soil, and a gas called carbon dioxide from the air, to create latex.

Latex travels up the tree through tiny capillary vessels, or tubes, in the bark. The *Hevea brasiliensis* tree produces more than 90 percent of the world's natural rubber.

Tree Tapping

A tree is ready to be tapped for latex when it is about six or seven years old. Rubber trees produce latex for about 25 to 30 years. Each tree can produce up to four gallons (15 liters) of latex per year. Latex flows for a short time until it begins to coagulate, or thicken into a solid. Solid latex is called rubber. Latex thickens when it is exposed to air, and eventually stops flowing. The tree then needs to "rest" before it can be tapped again.

(above) Workers on a rubber plantation in Con Thien, Vietnam, carry buckets of latex rubber. The latex has been tapped from trees planted in straight rows.

Wild Rubber

The rubber tree grows to a height of about 100 feet (30 meters). It has a silvery trunk and its upper branches have small, shiny, dark green leaves. Twice a year, the treetops produce small, yellow blossoms. After the flowers fall off, seed pods appear. In rainforests, the ripe pods explode with a loud bang, scattering seeds 100 feet (30 meters) away onto the forest floor. Within two to three weeks after landing on the soil, seedlings start to grow. Scattering the seeds is a natural defense the tree developed to protect itself against leaf blight. In the Amazon rainforest, leaf blight easily spreads between rubber trees that grow too close together, and the trees eventually die.

▲ *Seeds from the rubber tree. The seeds naturally scatter on the Amazon forest floor.*

To transport rubber more easily, a ball is made when heated latex hardens on a stick. Scientists believe hardened latex is used by rubber trees to cover wounds that appear in the bark.

Latex from Dandelions?

Thousands of other plants, such as the poinsettia and the fig plant, also produce latex. The latex in these plants and shrubs often contain a **resin** that has to be removed before the rubber can be used. The guayule shrub that grows in the dry sand of Mexico and the southwestern United States, and Russian dandelions are other latex-producing plants. Attempts have been made to try to gather enough latex from these plants to use in manufacturing, but this proved too time-consuming and costly for the amount of latex they produce.

Plantation and Laboratory

⊙⊙⊙⊙⊙⊙⊙⊙⊙⊙⊙⊙⊙⊙⊙⊙⊙⊙⊙⊙⊙⊙⊙⊙⊙

In Asian and African countries, rubber trees are grown on plantations. Plantations are large farms that often grow only one type of crop and whose workers usually live permanently on the farms. Seeds planted on plantations are specially treated to try to make the trees safe from diseases. Other measures are also used on plantations to protect the trees and make growing them as profitable as possible for the plantation owners. For example, seeds are often planted in nurseries and **grafted** to produce the best trees. About 100 trees are planted per acre (0.4 hectare). Trees planted closer together and in straight lines on plantations take less time to tap than those that grow wild.

(left) A woman worker taps a rubber tree on a modern rubber plantation in Malaysia.

(above) A rubber plantation manager in Malaysia relaxes with a gun at his side in the late 1940s. During this time, rebels fighting for their country's independence were attacking plantations.

Synthetic Rubber

Synthetic rubber is artificial, or human-made rubber. It was developed in World War II when natural rubber was in short supply. Synthetic rubber is made out of **petroleum** products, including a chemical called acetylene. Synthetic rubbers are made in a laboratory by chemists, or scientists who study chemicals. These rubbers are created to suit a specific need, and are often better suited to that purpose than natural rubber.

▼ ▶ Styrene butadiene rubber, or SBR, is the most common type of synthetic rubber used today. It is used mainly in tires. Synthetic rubber was developed for use on military vehicle tires and equipment during World War II when many natural rubber plantations in Asia were occupied, or taken over, by Japan.

The Native peoples of Amazonia were the first to use latex from rubber trees. Some Native peoples waterproofed their clothing by dipping them into latex. They also made waterproof shoes by dipping their feet into bowls of warm latex, and peeling the latex off their feet to allow it to harden. In Central America, the Native peoples mixed latex from the *Castilla elastica* tree with sap from a vine. When the mixture hardened, the rubber was shaped into the world's first bouncy balls.

Europe Demands Rubber

In 1495, Christopher Columbus arrived in Haiti with Spanish settlers to set up a **colony** in the **New World**. The settlers described seeing Native peoples play with balls made from the "gum of a tree." They had never seen such a substance before. For the next few hundred years, reports of rubber trickled back to Europe. Europeans were curious about rubber, but did not have much use for it. Some Europeans tried to copy the way the Native peoples of Central and South America used rubber latex to waterproof their clothing. It was difficult for Europeans to work with latex because it arrived in Europe in its solid form. This was because latex coagulates as soon as it is exposed to air. Once it was in its solid form, Europeans did not know how to make it a liquid again so that it could be shaped.

Sticky, Gooey, and Stinky

By experimenting with solid rubber, French scientists discovered how to make rubber liquid again in the 1760s. They used the chemical **turpentine** to dissolve the solid rubber back into liquid latex. With this discovery, Europeans could mold rubber into different shapes and harden them to form different objects. The first rubber tubing was made in Europe in 1770. By 1803, a rubber factory was opened in France to make rubber garters to hold up women's stockings.

In the early 1800s, demand for rubberized products, especially overshoes, rose in the United States. Manufacturers in North America and Europe invested a lot of money to open factories that made rubber products. They soon found that when their rubber goods were exposed to summer heat, they melted into a gooey, sticky, and stinky mess. In the cold of winter, rubber goods became hard and brittle.

▲ *Rubber was used at first, in products such as life preservers, garters and overshoes.*

(right) In 1823, Scottish chemist Charles Macintosh made waterproof cloth with rubber dissolved in a petroleum product called naptha. He sandwiched two layers of the naptha mixture between layers of fabric. This type of waterproof garment was called a macintosh. These women are wearing waterproof macintosh rain slickers from the 1930s.

Important Machines

Some Europeans and North Americans did not give up on rubber and kept on experimenting with it. British inventor Thomas Hancock opened England's first rubber factory in 1820. The factory made waterproof clothing for stagecoach passengers so their clothes stayed clean and dry while traveling. His factory also made rubber fasteners for clothing. Hancock invented a machine called a masticator that shredded rubber so that it could be reused. In Boston, Massachusetts, Edwin Chaffee opened the first rubber factory in the United States. He also invented a machine called a calender, for pressing rubber into smooth sheets. Chaffee's factory produced shoes, life preservers, and wagon covers from rubber.

Charles Goodyear

In 1839, an American named Charles Goodyear discovered a way to make rubber strong enough to withstand temperature changes. Through much trial and error, Goodyear found that when he accidentally dropped rubber mixed with **sulfur** on a hot stovetop, it became like leather but remained elastic. This developed into a process called vulcanization. Vulcanized rubber is harder and more durable and was soon used by manufacturers.

Early Rubber Tires

The invention of vulcanized rubber started a huge demand for the product. By 1870, rubber was needed for parts such as valves, washers, and pumps used in trains and factory machines. In the 1840s, Robert Thomson, an Englishman, created what was called an "elastic belt." It was a rubberized canvas tube filled with air and attached to a carriage wheel to give a smoother ride. Then, in 1887, John Boyd Dunlop, a Scotsman living in Ireland, invented a rubber tire for his son's tricycle. Cycling was a popular pastime in Europe and North America, and all early bikes had three wheels. The tire was made by cementing the ends of a rubber tube together, attaching a baby bottle nipple, and filling the tube with air. With their separate inventions, Thomson and Dunlop had created the pneumatic tire, or inflated rubber tire.

▲ *The Goodyear Tire and Rubber Company is one of the largest tire and rubber companies in the world, and is based in Akron, Ohio.*

(left) Charles Goodyear invented a process called vulcanization, which made rubber more durable and useful.

Better and Better Tires

Automobiles were invented in the late 1800s. By 1897, tires made from natural rubber with treads for gripping were being used instead of earlier smooth tires. In 1918, carbon black was added to tires. Carbon black is finely powdered, pure carbon that makes tires stronger and longer lasting. It also turns rubber from dark brown to black. The enormous popularity of automobiles, especially in North America, caused a boom in the rubber industry. Rubber companies that specialized in tires grew and prospered. Natural rubber was in greater demand than ever before. The main tire companies in the United States were the United States Rubber Company, Firestone, B.F. Goodrich, and Goodyear, which was not Charles Goodyear's company.

(above) In May, 1851, at the Great Expedition in London, England, Goodyear built a three-room display in which everything, including the furniture and curtains, was made of rubber.

Patents and Inventions

Inventors can apply for and receive a patent for their inventions. A patent is a government license that recognizes a person as the inventor or discoverer and gives him or her the sole right to make, use, or sell the invention. Charles Goodyear received his patent for vulcanization on June 15, 1844, nearly five years after inventing vulcanized rubber. Patents are meant to protect inventors so that only they receive profits from their discoveries. Sometimes, people copy inventions and try to claim them as their own or sell them for a profit. In these cases, the inventor must take the other person to court. Goodyear did this in a famous court case called "the Great India Rubber Case," which he won.

The Rubber Barons

While Europeans and North Americans made rubber products, the people supplying the rubber were the rubber barons of South America. From the late 1700s until 1912, the main source of rubber was Amazonia, where trees grew wild in the rainforest. Realizing the potential to make a lot of money as the main suppliers of the raw material, European, American, and South American businessmen of European descent started rubber companies. The rubber barons bought large areas of land in the rainforest along the Amazon River and the rivers that drain into it. The river was important because it was the only way to ship the rubber out of the Amazon, which they did on company-owned steamships. There were no roads or railways through the rainforest.

(above) Brazilian rubber tappers lived in thatched-roof shelters in the Amazon. Their lives were controlled by the rubber barons.

Rubber Monopoly

The rubber barons had a **monopoly** on rubber and sometimes fought one another for land. They needed the rubber extracted from the trees, which the Native peoples of the Amazon rainforest knew how to do. Rubber companies sent armed men on raids into the rainforest to capture and enslave the people living there. The Native peoples of Amazonia, such as the Boras, Andokes, Ocainas, and Huitotos, suffered terribly at the hands of the rubber barons.

Jungle Life

The rubber barons built trading posts and villages for workers in the rainforest, which were far from major cities. Tappers and slaves found everything needed for survival in the rainforest or through the rubber barons. The rubber barons hired armed men to control the tappers. Rubber barons in the city of Para, at the mouth of the Amazon River in Brazil, sold the rubber for enormous profit.

Rainforest Luxuries

While Native slaves and rubber tappers worked, rubber barons and their families lived in the luxury of cities they built in the jungle, such as Manaus in Brazil and Iquitos in Peru. The cities were boom towns, which meant they were built and grew during the high demand for rubber. Rubber barons paid high prices to import luxury goods from Europe, such as the finest foods, wine, clothing, and furniture. Sometimes even whole buildings were imported from Europe.

The Rubber Crash

The grand life of the rubber barons and their families ended in 1912 when rubber began to be produced in Southeast Asia. The rubber barons lost their monopoly on the supply of rubber and many returned to Europe, abandoning their land in Amazonia and the great cities they had built in the jungle.

(above) Native peoples who once harvested rubber in their rainforest homes, were later used as slaves on Amazon rubber plantations.

Paris of the Jungle

Rubber barons flaunted their wealth by building the city of Manaus deep in the rainforest. Here, where the Amazon River meets the Rio Negro, they built Brazil's first telephone system, 16 miles (26 kilometers) of streetcar, and an electric grid for a city three times its actual size. Manaus also boasted schools, libraries, a zoo, and an **ornate** opera house where European stars of the day performed.

Botanists, Colonists, and Thieves

The mid- to late 1700s was a period of exploration and colonization for European countries. They expanded their territories by building colonies in other lands. These colonies brought wealth to Europe in the form of natural resources. Countries such as Spain, Britain, France, Belgium, and the Netherlands set up colonies in Asia, Africa, and the Americas.

British Empire

Britain built an empire based on wealth from the sale of resources or raw materials found in its colonies, such as furs, fish, and timber. The resources were shipped from the colony back to Britain and manufactured into products. The products, such as beaver felt hats, were then sold back to the colonies and to other countries. In the 1700s, Britain began looking for plants, such as rubber, to **cultivate** in its colonies and sell for profit. By the 1800s, the world demand for rubber was so great that Britain decided it wanted to grow rubber in its tropical colonies. Growing rubber meant that Britain would have control over its supply and not be dependent on Brazil, a foreign supplier and Portuguese colony.

English planter Henry Wickham broke the Amazonian monopoly of the rubber industry. He brought rubber seeds to England. The seeds were then sent to the botanical gardens in the British colonies of Ceylon (later Sri Lanka), Indonesia, and Singapore. Rubber plantations then spread throughout the world.

South American Expedition

In 1735, France's Academy of Sciences sent an expedition to gather plants in South America. In Ecuador, the expedition gathered rubber samples and wrote a report telling how the Native peoples of the Amazon processed and used latex. The report caught the attention of **botanists** throughout Europe. At the time, many botonists were organizing expeditions to gather, classify, and name plants from around the globe. Other botonists were sent out to colonies to see what kinds of profitable plants they could find.

18

(above) Plantation workers in Malaysia packed sheet rubber to be sent back to England and made into products.

Wickham and the Theft

In order to grow its own supply of rubber, the British government decided it had to steal rubber plants from Amazonia, where they were closely guarded. In 1873, Henry Wickham, an English planter living in South America, was hired to take *Hevea* seeds out of Amazonia. Wickham then hired Native peoples in the Amazon to gather seeds from the forest floor. For the operation to be a success, Wickham had to get the seeds out of Brazil secretly and quickly so they would survive until they could be planted in **greenhouses** in England. Of the 70,000 seeds taken, only 2,500 survived.

To Asia!

The seedlings from English greenhouses were transplanted to British colonial plantations in Southeast Asia. Plantation owners grew tea and coffee in Malaysia and were not easily convinced to grow rubber instead. Two coffee growers agreed to plant five acres (two hectares) of rubber trees in western Malaysia. It was the first successful rubber plantation in Southeast Asia. Twelve years later, more than 740,000 acres (300,000 hectares) of rubber trees grew in Sri Lanka and Malaysia. By the beginning of the 1900s, Dutch planters established plantations in Indonesia. By 1914, Southeast Asia was supplying rubber to European manufacturers.

◀ Christian missionaries went to the Congo to convert the Congolese to Christianity. Many missionaries were shocked when they saw the brutal treatment of the Congolese rubber tappers. Tappers, or their family members, had their hands cut off by plantation owners as punishment when the owners felt the tappers were not harvesting enough latex. The missionaries took pictures to make outsiders aware of what was going on.

A King's Colony

The British were not alone in wanting to build an empire. Belgium's king, Leopold II, wanted to establish his own empire. He did this by gaining control of the Congo, a large area of land in central Africa. In 1885, he convinced Congolese village chiefs to sign treaties, or agreements, which gave him the rights to the land. Under his rule, the people of the Congo could only trade with Belgian companies, which paid Leopold 50 percent of their profits. In the mid-1890s, the rubber boom hit. The Congo was rich in a supply of rubber gathered from the *Landophia* vine, which is a plant native to the Congo's rainforest.

▶ Latex for rubber in the Congo came from a vine that grew in the country's rainforest.

Terror in the Congo

To make as much money as he could from rubber, King Leopold imposed a special tax to be paid by village chiefs. The tax was in the form of slaves, who were used to gather rubber. The Congolese were sold into slavery to work as rubber tappers. They were forced to gather a certain amount of latex each day, called a quota. To try to meet large quotas, Congolese slaves started slashing the vines too deep to get more latex, killing the vine. This meant they had to go even deeper into the swampy forests each day to reach vines so they could fill their next quota.

Sometimes, a Congolese rubber tapper would be gone away from home for as many as 24 days a month. A failure to meet a quota was severely punished. Some tappers' wives and children were held hostage or the hands of their children or family members were cut off.

▶ *Rubber boots are perfect for farm work.*

Edison's Rubber Experiment

▼ *Thomas Edison worked with Henry Ford, the carmaker, and Harvey Firestone, the tire maker, both of whom had created companies that greatly depended on rubber.*

The United States also tried to establish its own rubber supply. In the 1920s, American inventor Thomas Edison did not believe that the United States should be dependent on foreign supplies of rubber and he began to search for a rubber plant that could grow in tropical North American climates, such as in the state of Florida. Edison built a ten-acre (four-hectare) experimental garden in Florida and hired botanists to find plants around the Gulf that could produce rubber. Edison tried growing the guayule plant, a latex-producing shrub from Central Mexico. The latex of the guayule plant is encased in special cells of the plant, and does not run through the trees as it does in the rubber tree. In the end, extracting the latex proved to take too long and be too expensive a process for the small amount of rubber that it produced.

Filling a Need

Countries that did not have their own supply of rubber from their colonies had to depend on foreign suppliers. As rubber became important for automobiles and in manufacturing, scientists worked to create an artificial rubber with the same qualities as natural rubber, that could be used in place of natural rubber.

World War I

Germany was one of the first countries to try to create synthetic rubber. During World War I, when Britain and Germany were enemies, Britain controlled most of the rubber supply from Southeast Asia. When Britain cut off Germany's rubber supply, Germany **confiscated** all the rubber in the country, such as bicycle and car tires, to use for weapons and war vehicles. German scientists made a synthetic rubber from coal and lime, called methyl rubber. Methyl rubber froze and broke apart in cold weather. After the war, Germany stopped producing methyl rubber, but scientists continued their research to develop better synthetic rubbers.

Early Attempts

In 1931, American chemist Wallace Carothers created a synthetic rubber called neoprene by working with Du Pont, an American chemical company. Neoprene was considered the first successful synthetic rubber. By 1934, it was used to make tires. Unfortunately, Du Pont's neoprene factory exploded and neoprene went off the market. Carothers' discovery led to the invention of nylon, a synthetic fabric.

Germany's Rubber

As World War II approached, Germany again grew desperate for rubber. German researchers worked with the Standard Oil Company in the United States to create Buna rubber in 1932. Buna rubber has similar properties to natural rubber and was used by manufacturers in the United States to replace neoprene.

(above) North Americans were encouraged by their governments to donate their rubber goods to be recycled for use in the war. Children often went from house to house, collecting old bicycle tires and rubber boots for the cause.

War Demands Rubber!

By the start of World War II in 1939, rubber was being used for much more than just tires. Each military vehicle contained about 300 rubber parts. This high demand for rubber for the war effort was being met mostly by rubber plantations in Southeast Asia. In 1942, Japan invaded the natural rubber producing countries of the Pacific, including Indonesia. This stopped the supply of rubber from reaching the **Allies**, who were fighting against Japan in the war. The creation of Butyl rubber, which developed from the invention of Buna rubber, came at the same time that the natural rubber supply was cut off.

Roosevelt's Rubber Plan

The Allies looked to the United States to meet their rubber needs. Even before the United States had officially entered World War II, U.S. president Franklin Roosevelt set up the Rubber Reserve Company to **stockpile** rubber and control its use. The American companies Standard Oil, Firestone, BF Goodrich, Goodyear, and U.S. Rubber, were ordered to work together to make improvements to rubber. At the end of World War II, natural rubber became available again, but the synthetics industry had been born. By the 1950s, more synthetic rubber was being used than natural rubber.

▶ *Natural and synthetic rubbers are made of isoprene, a product of petroleum.*

(above) This American cartoon from 1942 depicts the addition of rubber tires to the goods that were rationed, or had their use limited, during World War II. Many commodities were rationed because they were in short supply.

Oil and Tires

In 1973, the price of petroleum, the main ingredient for making synthetic rubber, rose. At the same time, the use of the **radial tire** was growing in North America. Radial tires were invented in France in the 1940s. They needed the sturdiness that only natural rubber provides. Synthetic rubber is the most widely used rubber today, but scientists have not yet come up with a synthetic that can replace natural rubber entirely.

23

Tappers and Plantations

Rubber tappers are people who extract latex from rubber trees to make natural rubber. Tappers in Brazil and other parts of Amazonia tap trees in the rainforests that grow wild. In Asia and Africa, rubber tappers work on plantations, where trees are planted and grow close together in rows.

Brazilian Rubber Tappers

During the rubber boom of the late 1800s in South America, thousands of workers from northeast Brazil moved to Amazonia to tap rubber. The workers were in debt, or owed money, to rubber barons for having paid their way to Amazonia. Their debt mounted as the rubber barons supplied their food, clothing, shelter, and tools at high cost. It was nearly impossible for tappers to escape debt because the rubber barons paid them such low wages.

Henry Ford's Brazilian Plantation

In 1927, carmaker Henry Ford bought over two million acres (800,000 hectares) of land in northern Brazil to build his own rubber plantation called Fordlandia. Ford wanted to ensure a steady and inexpensive supply of rubber for the United States, and for his own car company. Steel, cement, trains, medicine, food, houses for workers, and storage buildings were brought from America to establish a plantation. Fordlandia also had a hospital, schools, clubs, a tennis court, a golf course, and an experimental laboratory. The overseers on the plantation were Americans who hired local workers to plant over one million rubber trees.

(above) Brazilian rubber tappers planting rubber trees on Henry Ford's plantation, Fordlandia.

Cafeteria Riot

Ford's Brazilian tappers were required to live separately from their families in barracks built on the plantations. They worked 11-hour days and had little control over their lives. In December 1930, the tappers went on **strike**. Workers demanded the right to go to river ports without passes and to be allowed off the plantations. The Brazilian military ended the strike, and many tappers were arrested. In 1934, the Fordlandia plantation was abandoned after leaf blight killed the closely-planted rubber trees.

Plantation Workers

In the early 1900s, rubber plantations were set up by colonists in Malaysia, Burma, India, Sri Lanka, and Indonesia. People living there were hired to tap the trees and **indentured laborers** were brought from India and China. Their passage to the plantation was paid, and they were given food and shelter, but they were not paid wages.

(right) Processing latex the old-fashioned way.

Second Wave

During World War II, more rubber tappers moved to the Amazon as the American demand for rubber increased. The tappers worked for small rubber traders. In the 1970s, the Brazilian government began to sell areas of the rainforest to cattle ranchers and logging companies, who moved into the rainforests and cleared the land. After much protest from tappers and others, the Brazilian government set up "extraction reserves," in 1985, which protected certain areas of the forest from development.

Chico Mendes and the Rubber Union

Chico Mendes was a Brazilian rubber tapper who organized rubber tappers into a union called the National Council of Rubber Tappers. A union is a group of workers who unite to protect their rights. The union struggled to help free tappers from the debt they owed to the rubber traders. It also fought to save the rainforest trees from being cleared by cattle ranchers who wanted to take over the land for farming.

Chico Mendes (1944-1988) was a Brazilian rubber tapper who tried to save the rainforest and his livelihood. He was shot to death in 1988 by cattle ranchers angry with his work.

From Latex to Rubber

Wild rubber trees in Amazonia grow far apart. Tappers clear paths through the forest to the trees. To prepare the trees, the top layer of bark is scraped away to a smooth, flat surface. Days later, a shallow diagonal cut is made in the bark around the tree. Latex leaks out of the tree and flows into a bucket below the cut. Rubber tree bark cannot be cut too deeply or the tree will be damaged. The same part of a tree can only be tapped two or three times. Once the bark has regrown, cuts are made in the opposite direction. Tappers cut the bark each morning and return later to collect the buckets.

By this time, the latex has coagulated and the flow has stopped. Sometimes a chemical is added to the bark to prevent coagulation and the latex continues to flow into large containers that are emptied every few days.

Smoking the Rubber

Smoking was once the main way of making rubber in Amazonia. Tappers took latex to jungle smoking huts where cacao pods were burned in clay ovens to create smoke. The rubber tappers held poles over large vats of hot latex. Latex was scooped out of the vats and continuously poured over the poles. The latex hardened into a 200-pound (90-kilogram) ball. Smoking turned the white latex into dark brown rubber.

What A Sap

Today, latex is often hardened using the sap of the Amazonian ofe tree. Latex is poured into a box, then the ofe sap is added. The box is covered and the latex inside sets into a solid rubber block that weighs about 90 pounds (40 kilograms).

Plantation Rubber

On plantations, latex is poured through a **sieve** to strain the dirt, bark, and leaves from it. The latex is mixed in a large tank. Chemicals are added to preserve the rubber and the latex is then processed in a large tank that spins at a high speed. The latex forms solid rubber and is shipped to factories for further processing.

(above) Rubber duckies are now mostly made from plastic.

In the Amazon, latex is sometimes still smoked into large balls then pressed into sheets.

Firestone's African Plantation

In 1926, the American-owned tire company, Firestone, signed an agreement with the government of Liberia, in Africa, for rubber plantation land. Firestone spent five million dollars for a 99-year lease on one million acres (404,700 hectares) of land. The plantation was named Harbel, after Firestone's owners at the time, Harvey Firestone and his wife, Idabelle. Harbel was an important rubber supplier to America during World War II. Today, the plantation still employs many Liberians. Workers are paid low wages, but depend on their work on the plantation to survive. Liberia is a poor nation which has recently suffered through years of **civil war**.

A Liberian soldier guards the Firestone plantation in Liberia, Africa. Rubber is important to the country's economy.

Recycling and Reusing

◎◎◎◎◎◎◎◎◎◎◎◎◎◎◎◎◎◎◎◎◎◎◎◎◎

Natural rubber used to decompose, or rot, but so many chemicals are now added to natural rubber during processing that it will no longer decompose. Synthetic rubber is made from chemicals that do not easily break down. There are billions of used rubber tires throughout the world. Disposing of these used tires is a problem. Once the tires have been vulcanized, they cannot be melted down easily for reuse. In some countries, old tires are cut up and used to make shoes and sandals. Scientists are experimenting with ways to devulcanize tires.

New Tires from Old Tires

Tire re-treading is one way to cut back on the number of tires being made. In re-treading, a new layer of rubber treads is attached to the old tire, instead of completely replacing the tire. Re-treading is mostly done on large truck tires. In other cases, old tires are shredded and made into a dust that is mixed with asphalt to make roads. Roads paved with asphalt containing rubber are more waterproof than other roads. This mixture lasts longer on roads, but is hard to work with and is harmful to the road crew's health.

People have come up with some clever ways of reusing tires that are no longer suitable for vehicles. Starting in the 1970s, tires were weighed down and sunk to the bottom of the ocean. Over time, the tires became an artificial reef encrusted with sea animals that attract fish and other sea life.

The Future

New uses for rubber and new, more specialized rubbers are being created every day. Companies hire chemists to design new kinds of rubber. Their formulas are guarded very closely so that other companies cannot make them too. One new use for natural rubber is earthquake proofing for buildings. In areas prone to earthquakes, such as Tokyo and San Francisco, natural rubber in latex form is added to building foundations. The latex foundations allow buildings to sway and not topple with the Earth's shaking during a quake.

▼ *This shoulder bag was made from recycled rubber tire inner tubes.*

Tire Fire!

Sometimes, people set fire to old tires. Burning tires creates harmful chemicals called dioxins, that are released into the air. Dioxins are harmful gases that can cause birth defects and diseases such as cancer in humans. Tire fires cannot be put out by water because of the toxic, or poisonous runoff that is created. People living close to the fire are evacuated from their homes because of the black, **acrid** smoke. In Ohio in 1999, a massive tire fire was set by arsonists, or people who start fires on purpose. The tire fire cost the state more than three million dollars to clean up.

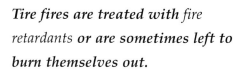

Tire fires are treated with fire retardants *or are sometimes left to burn themselves out.*

Rubber Today

Rubber is unlike any other substance. Rubber can be made into a firm foam or used to coat products, such as dolls and gloves. It can be rolled into sheets or made into threads. It can be bonded with metals or woven with nylon or polyester to make stretchy fabric. Rubber is waterproof and airtight. It can be sterilized and used in medical supplies. Just about the only thing you cannot do with rubber is eat it!

Tires and Industry

The main use of rubber today is in the transportation industry, especially for making tires and tubes. Rubber is used to make equipment such as hoses, conveyor belts, and glues. Aircraft tires are made almost entirely of natural rubber because it is so strong. Almost three-quarters of all natural rubber produced today is used to make tires.

Rubber Entertainment

From Halloween masks to the dinosaurs of the Jurassic Park films, rubber is widely used for special effects. Masks are made by pouring latex into clay or plaster molds and allowing the latex to set, before peeling it out. The skin of the giant dinosaurs of Jurassic Park was made from foam rubber, which is latex mixed with air to make it spongy.

▲ Rubber chickens have been joke-shop favorites for many years.

▸ Fantastic creatures, such as Jedi master Yoda from the original Star Wars trilogy, are made from rubber.

To help the whole family *sleep well.*

WESTBROOK & THOMPSON LTD.,
101 Southwark Bridge Road, LONDON, S.E.1

▲ Hot water bottles are soft rubber containers that are used to soothe people during illnesses.

Rubber Clothes

Rubber is used in the clothing industry. Underpants stay up because of a rubber elastic around the waistband. Elastic is made from latex threads that are woven into a cloth to make a continuous strip. During World War II, a stretchy thread called spandex was created. Spandex is a strong, flexible, stretchy material that is perfect for sports clothes and swimsuits. Before latex and spandex, swimsuits were made of heavy wool that stretched and shrunk out of shape. Rubber also replaced the metal, bones, and heavy lacing used to give clothing shape from the 1800s to the 1900s.

▸ *A drawing of a "cholera preventive costume" from the 1800s, showing a man wearing a bulky rubber costume. Cholera was a disease that people did not yet know how to prevent.*

(above) Foam rubber was invented in 1929. It is a latex froth, or latex that is mixed with millions of tiny bubbles. The development of foam rubber allowed toy makers to create bendable toys.

Glossary

acrid Having a strong and unpleasant smell

Allies The nations that fought together in World War II, including Britain, France, the United States, and the Soviet Union

botanist A scientist who studies plants

Christian A follower of the teachings of Jesus Christ

civil war A war between two groups within one country or culture

colony Land ruled by another country

confiscate To seize property with authority

cultivate To farm and harvest a crop

durability A strong material that does not wear down easily

fire retardant A material that does not burn

greenhouse A glass room or building used to grow plants that need a warm temperature

graft To join a plant, bud, or shoot to another plant so that they grow together as a single plant

indentured laborer Someone, bound by contract, to work for someone else for a period of time

monopoly Control over a commodity

New World The name given to North, Central, and South America by Europeans

nutrients Substances that help living things grow

ornate Decorated beautifully with great detail

petroleum A dark liquid found underground that is used to create gasoline and other fuels

radial tire A tire used by most cars today, that is more flexible and durable than earlier tires and has been proven to help a car decrease the amount of gas it uses.

resin A sticky, strong-smelling substance that oozes from the bark and wood of many trees

sieve A device used to separate smaller particles from larger particles

spore A type of cell produced by fungi that can grow and become a fully developed fungus

stockpile To collect a large amount of goods

strike When employees stop work in order to get better working conditions

sulfur A yellow-colored chemical

tropical A region that has a hot climate with little change between seasons

turpentine An oil from the wood or resin of certain pine trees

Index

1 2 3 4 5 6 7 8 9 0 Printed in the U.S.A. 4 3 2 1 0 9 8 7 6 5